FIX THE HICCUPS

Written by Dale Tenby
Illustrated by Laetitia Aynie

Sal, Jas and I have tickets
to go on the Rocket.
Sal has hiccups.

The Rocket will fix her hiccups.

We get into the Rocket.
The man hits the button.

The Rocket zigzags.
The Rocket is quick.

Up, up, up! We get to the top.

The Rocket dips to the bottom.

Did the Rocket fix Sal's hiccups?
Yes, but Jas and I are sick!